CRAFTING WITH NATURE

LEAF
CRAFTS

BY REBECCA SABELKO

Express!

BELLWETHER MEDIA · MINNEAPOLIS, MN

Imagination comes alive in **Express!**
Transform the everyday into the fresh and new,
discover ways to stir up flavor and excitement,
and experiment with new ideas and materials.
Express! makerspace books: where your next
creative adventure begins!

This edition first published in 2020 by Bellwether Media, Inc.

No part of this publication may be reproduced in whole or in part without written permission of the publisher.
For information regarding permission, write to Bellwether Media, Inc., Attention: Permissions Department,
6012 Blue Circle Drive, Minnetonka, MN 55343.

Library of Congress Cataloging-in-Publication Data

Names: Rebecca Sabelko, author.

LC record for Leaf Crafts available at https://lccn.loc.gov/2019035129

Text copyright © 2020 by Bellwether Media, Inc. BLASTOFF! READERS and associated logos are trademarks
and/or registered trademarks of Bellwether Media, Inc.

Editor: Betsy Rathburn   Designer: Andrea Schneider

Printed in the United States of America, North Mankato, MN.

Table of Contents

Crafting with Nature

DECIDUOUS TREES

CONIFEROUS TREES

Leaves help plants stay alive! Leafy plants are found all over the world.

Some are **deciduous**. Their leaves change colors and fall off. The plants go **dormant** during the cold winter months. Others are **coniferous**. These evergreens keep their color year-round!

Common Poisonous Leaves in the United States

Avoid these leaves as you collect materials.

 POISON IVY

 POISON OAK

 POISON SUMAC

Nature Safety

- ✘ Have an adult check the area for any dangerous plants, animals, or other materials.

- ✘ Do not collect nature items from national or state parks.

- ✘ Ask permission to take items from yards or other private property.

- ✘ Stay away from animal nests and homes.

- ✘ Only collect as many supplies as needed.

Leaf Rubbings

All leaves have veins. They give leaves shape and support. Veins move water and **nutrients** in the leaf.

Leaf veins also help scientists study **climate change**. Research has shown that vein patterns that are closer together take in more **carbon**. This may help reduce the amount of carbon in the **atmosphere**. It could be a step toward reducing climate change!

TYPES OF VEINS

Some plants, such as palm trees, have a straight vein pattern. Other plants have a netlike pattern of veins. This pattern is common in maple leaves.

a variety of leaves

white paper

tape

crayons

With the leaves' undersides facing up, place the paper over the leaves. Tape the corners down.

Rub the paper with the side of the crayon. You will begin to see the details of the leaves on the paper. Use as many colors as you want!

Remove the wrapping on the crayons.

When the paper is filled, remove the tape and the leaves. Add designs to your work of art!

Leaf Hedgehog

1 Paint the bottom of the paper plate brown. Let the paint dry completely.

2 Cut the paper plate in half.

3

With the brown sides facing out, glue the halves together along the round edge. Leave the straight edge open.

Hedgehogs are small **mammals** found in Europe, Africa, and Asia. They are covered in a coat of stiff spines. Hedgehogs use these as defense against **predators**. They curl up into a tight, spiny ball, warning their enemies to stay away!

Hedgehogs are active at night. They spend their days sleeping. At night, they use their senses of smell and hearing to find food.

materials

paper plate

brown paint

10 to 20 fresh, fake, or dried leaves

glue

ALL in ThE NAME

Hedgehogs get their name from their hunting behavior. They often make a piglike sound while searching for food under hedges.

Lay the paper plate so the flat edge is facing you. Glue leaves onto the paper plate starting with the left side. Overlap leaves to avoid gaps.

5 Once the left side is filled with leaves, add one more row. Create a rounded edge to give the hedgehog's head shape.

6 Glue the googly eye to the hedgehog's head. Use the marker to add a nose.

7 Repeat the steps on the other side of the paper plate. Your hedgehog is ready to display!

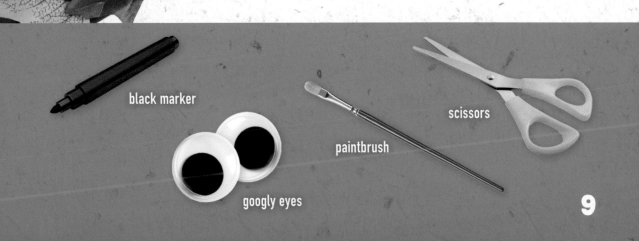

black marker

googly eyes

paintbrush

scissors

Leaf DreamCatcher

1 Cut the leaves into small pieces.

2 Paint a thin layer of craft glue on one side of the plastic lid.

Dreamcatchers were first created by the Ojibwe people. These sacred hoops served as a way to move good dreams back to the dreamer.

Ojibwe dreamcatchers were made from willow twigs, animal **sinew**, and feathers. Bad dreams were caught in the web. Good dreams passed through the center hole. The bad dreams passed away as morning arrived.

3

Place the leaf pieces onto the glue. Explore different patterns, shapes, and designs.

materials

glue

flat leaves

scissors

plastic lid

4 When the glue is dry, add another thin layer. Allow it to dry.

An AdOPTEd PraCTiCE

Later on, other native groups adopted the use of dreamcatchers. They added their own unique touches with beads and gemstones as well as other materials.

5

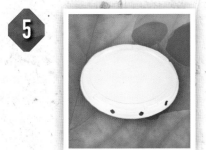

Punch three holes about 1.5 inches (4 centimeters) apart along the bottom of the lid.

6 Thread a piece of string through each of the three bottom holes. Secure them to the plastic lid with a knot.

7 Tie leaves, beads, and feathers to each string.

8 Punch one hole through the top of the plastic lid, directly across from the middle hole at the bottom of the lid. Thread a piece of string through the hole and tie together. Your dreamcatcher is ready to hang!

beads and feathers

hole punch

4 pieces of string, each at least 24 inches (61 centimeters) long

paintbrush

11

Leaf Wall Hanging

North America has many different **biomes**. Each is home to different types of trees. Oak, maple, and beech trees are common in the deciduous forests of the eastern United States. Coniferous pine and spruce forests span across Canada.

The **rain forests** of the northwestern United States are home to large western hemlocks. In the tropics, kapok and ramón trees grow in the rain forests.

TOWERING TREES

Rain forests have three or four layers. The top is the canopy. It can reach over 300 feet (91 meters) high!

materials

1 stick about 32 inches (81 centimeters) long

scissors

fresh, dried, or fake leaves

beads or feathers

24 long pieces of string

1

Make a mark 4 inches (10 centimeters) from each end of the stick. These are the starting and ending points for the strings.

2

Beginning at the starting mark, tie long pieces of string 1 inch (3 centimeters) apart. Make each string a different length. Continue until you reach the ending mark.

3

Once you reach the ending mark, tie a leaf to the end of each string. Feel free to add feathers, beads, or other items. Use your wall hanging to decorate your home!

CRAFT TiP

Use clear fishing line to make the leaves look like they are floating!

Leaf CroWn

Ancient Egyptians used the papyrus plant in many different ways. The plant is known for its use in making paper. But it was also turned into rope, sandals, toys, and much more!

The palm is another plant that has been used for centuries. The leaves can be made into housing material and clothing, especially hats!

A NAturAL PASt

Papyrus was used to make paper for many centuries. In time, parchment paper became more common. This paper is made from animal skins!

PAPYRUS PLANTS

fresh leaves, flowers, sticks, and other natural materials

craft wire

floral tape

wire cutters

1 Use the wire cutters to carefully cut a piece of wire long enough to go around your head. Add 2 to 3 inches (5 to 8 centimeters).

3 Select your first leaf and attach the stem to the wire with a small piece of floral tape.

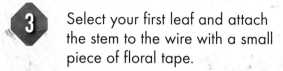

2

Bend the wire into a circle and twist the ends together.

4 Continue adding leaves, flowers, sticks, and other natural materials to the wire with floral tape. Wear your leaf crown for a special look!

Leaf Bowl

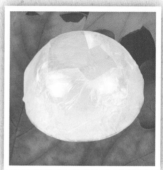

1

Cover the outside of the bowl with plastic wrap.

Papier-mâché was created in China around 200 BCE. Paper, water, and glue were layered to create helmets. Over time, papier-mâché was used in Japan to make masks.

Today, papier-mâché is used to make all kinds of arts and crafts. It is often used to make piñatas. It is also used to create festive floats in parades!

2

Paint a layer of glue onto the plastic. Place a leaf on the bowl, being careful to shape the leaf to the curve of the bowl.

PAPER BOATS!

In the 1800s, papier-mâché was used to make paper boats in America!

materials

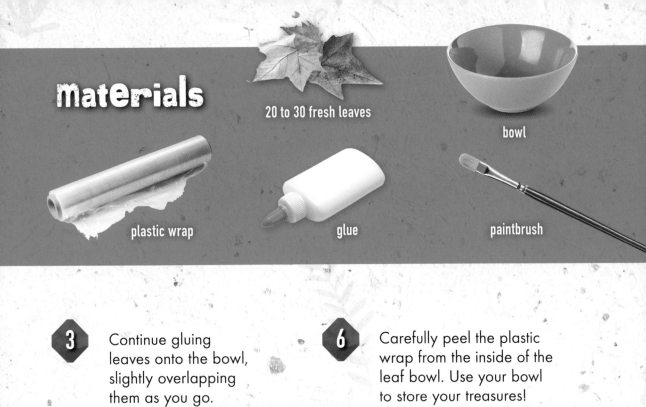

20 to 30 fresh leaves

bowl

plastic wrap

glue

paintbrush

3 Continue gluing leaves onto the bowl, slightly overlapping them as you go.

4 Once the bowl is covered in leaves, allow the glue to dry completely. Repeat steps 2 and 3 two more times.

5 Carefully lift the leaf bowl off of the mold bowl.

6 Carefully peel the plastic wrap from the inside of the leaf bowl. Use your bowl to store your treasures!

17

Leaf Roses

Roses have been popular flowers for centuries. People enjoy them for their beauty as well as what they **symbolize**. Each color carries a special meaning.

Red roses are one of the many symbols of love. They are often given for special occasions. Pink roses may be given to bring cheer or give thanks. Yellow roses represent joy and friendship.

A GARdEN OF ROSES

There are around 150 different types of roses found in nature!

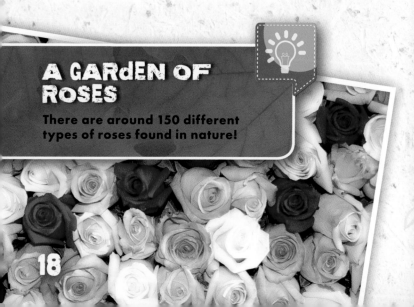

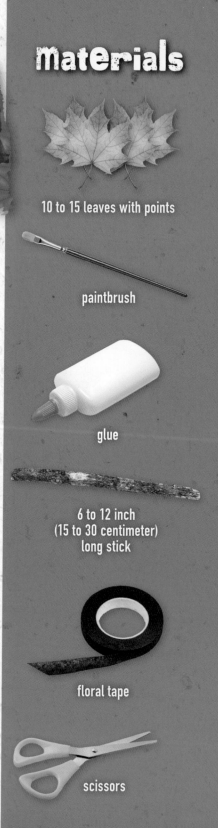

materials

10 to 15 leaves with points

paintbrush

glue

6 to 12 inch
(15 to 30 centimeter)
long stick

floral tape

scissors

Place a leaf so that its veins are facing up. Place a dot of glue on each point and fold in. Repeat with about 10 leaves.

Once the leaves are dry, roll one of the leaves into a spiral.

Stand the rolled leaf in the center of another leaf. Wrap both sides of the second leaf around the rolled leaf. Glue the second rolled leaf around the first rolled leaf.

Once you have the size you want, wrap the stems of the leaves tightly with floral tape.

Place a stick against the wrapped stems and wrap it with floral tape. Repeat the steps to make as many roses as you want!

Continue adding leaves, rotating the flower as you go to get an even size. Use larger leaves without folded points on the outside.

CRAFT TiP

Maple leaves are great for making leaf roses. The points on the leaves help make the roses look more realistic!

Leaf Weaving

The earliest weavings were fabrics, baskets, and nets dating back to 27,000 BCE. Materials such as twigs or animal hair were woven by some **nomadic** people to create shelter. Yarn was used to create clothing, sails, and much more!

Different types of weaving create different types of fabrics. Plain weaves create **muslin**. Twill weaves make denim. Pile weaves are used to make fabrics such as velvet and plush.

21ST CENTURY WEAVING

Today, most of the fabric used to make clothing is created on looms controlled by computers.

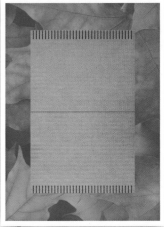

Draw a line at the center of an 8-inch side of the cardboard. From there, draw a line every 1/4 inches (0.6 centimeters) until you reach the outside edges. Repeat on the other 8-inch side.

Cut along each line on the top and bottom edges of the cardboard.

materials

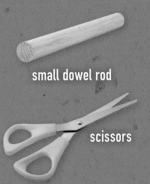

small dowel rod

8-inch by 11-inch
(20-centimeter by
28-centimeter) piece
of cardboard

twigs and flowers

strong string

scissors

ruler

a variety of leaves

pencil

3 Tie a knot at one end of your string. Place the knot at the back of the first tab on the bottom of the loom. Wrap the string or yarn around the loom, working it between each tab as you go. Once you reach the last tab, tie the string at the back of the loom.

5 Use the small leaves, twigs, and flowers to fill in space.

6 Carefully pull the loops of string off each tab. Once all the loops are free, cut the center of each loop and double knot the ends of the strings. Slide a dowel rod through the top loops. Use it to hang your leaf weaving!

4

Begin weaving leaves in front of and behind every other string on the loom. Continue until the loom is covered.

Glossary

atmosphere—the mass of air that surrounds the earth

biomes—large areas with certain plants, animals, and weather

carbon—an element found in nature

climate change—a human-caused change in Earth's weather due to warming temperatures

coniferous—relating to trees that make cones and have needles that usually stay green year-round

deciduous—relating to trees that have leaves that fall off every year

dormant—not active for a certain period of time

mammals—warm-blooded animals that have backbones and feed their young milk

muslin—a type of woven cotton fabric

nomadic—relating to people who have no fixed home but wander from place to place

nutrients—the things plants need to live and grow

papier-mâché—material made of paper mixed with glue and other substances that hardens as it dries

predators—animals that hunt other animals for food

rain forests—thick, green forests that receive a lot of rain

sinew—strong tissues that connect muscles to bones

symbolize—to stand for something else

to learn more

AT THE LIBRARY

Hickman, Pamela. *Nature All Around: Trees*. Boston, Mass.: Kids Can Press, 2019.

Rathburn, Betsy. *Stick Crafts*. Minneapolis, Minn.: Bellwether Media, 2020.

Socha, Piotr. *Trees: A Rooted History*. New York, N.Y.: Abrams Books for Young Readers, 2019.

ON THE WEB

FACTSURFER

Factsurfer.com gives you a safe, fun way to find more information.

1. Go to www.factsurfer.com.

2. Enter "leaf crafts" into the search box and click 🔍.

3. Select your book cover to see a list of related web sites.

index